LIGHTNING
BOLT
BOOKS™

Meet a Baby Ostrich

Marie Powell

Lerner Publications

Minneapolis

Content Consultant: Dr. Mark C. Andersen, Department of Fish Wildlife and Conservation Ecology, New Mexico State University

Lerner Publications Company
A division of Lerner Publishing Group, Inc.
241 First Avenue North
Minneapolis, MN 55401 USA

For reading levels and more information, look up this title at www.lernerbooks.com.

Library of Congress Cataloging-in-Publication Data

Powell, Marie, 1958-
     Meet a baby ostrich / Marie Powell.
        pages cm. — (Lightning Bolt Books™. Baby African animals)
     Includes index.
     Audience: Ages 5–8.
     Audience: Grades K to 3.
     ISBN 978-1-4677-7971-5 (lb : alk. paper) — ISBN 978-1-4677-8369-9 (pb : alk. paper) —
ISBN 978-1-4677-8370-5 (eb pdf)
     1. Ostriches—Juvenile literature. I. Title.
QL696.S9P69 2014
598.5'241392—dc23

                                                          2014038834

Manufactured in the United States of America
1 — BP — 7/15/15

Table of Contents

The Largest Egg — page 4

Growing and Changing — page 10

Let's Eat! — page 18

Home in the Savanna — page 24

Habitat in Focus — page 28

Fun Facts — page 29

Glossary — page 30

Further Reading — page 31

Index — page 32

The Largest Egg

It's almost time! Baby ostriches are about to hatch. The babies will be born in a big sand pit. A male ostrich dug the pit with his feet. Many mother ostriches laid their eggs there. This means lots of babies are on the way!

An ostrich pit can hold twelve to sixty eggs.

Each ostrich egg is about 7 inches (17 centimeters) long. And the eggs weigh around 3.5 pounds (1.6 kilograms). That's as much as twenty-four chicken eggs.

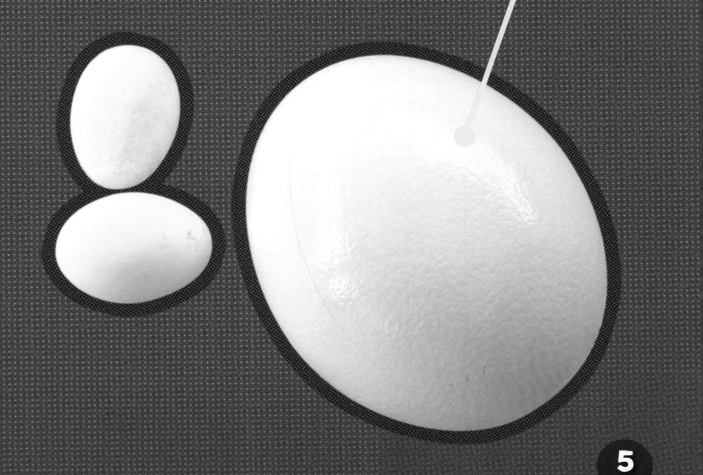

Ostrich eggs are the biggest bird eggs.

A female may lay her neck along the ground to hide while she sits on her eggs.

One female sits on the eggs during the day to keep them warm. The male sits on the eggs at night because his black and white feathers hide him in the dark.

After about six weeks, the baby ostriches begin to chirp inside the eggs. Their necks stiffen so they can break through the eggs' shells. Soon they push their way out.

Baby ostriches are called chicks.

Chicks are already 1 foot (30 cm) tall when they hatch. That's about as long as a ruler. Adult ostriches are 9 feet (3 meters) tall, or almost as tall as a basketball hoop.

Chicks will soon grow to be as tall as their parents.

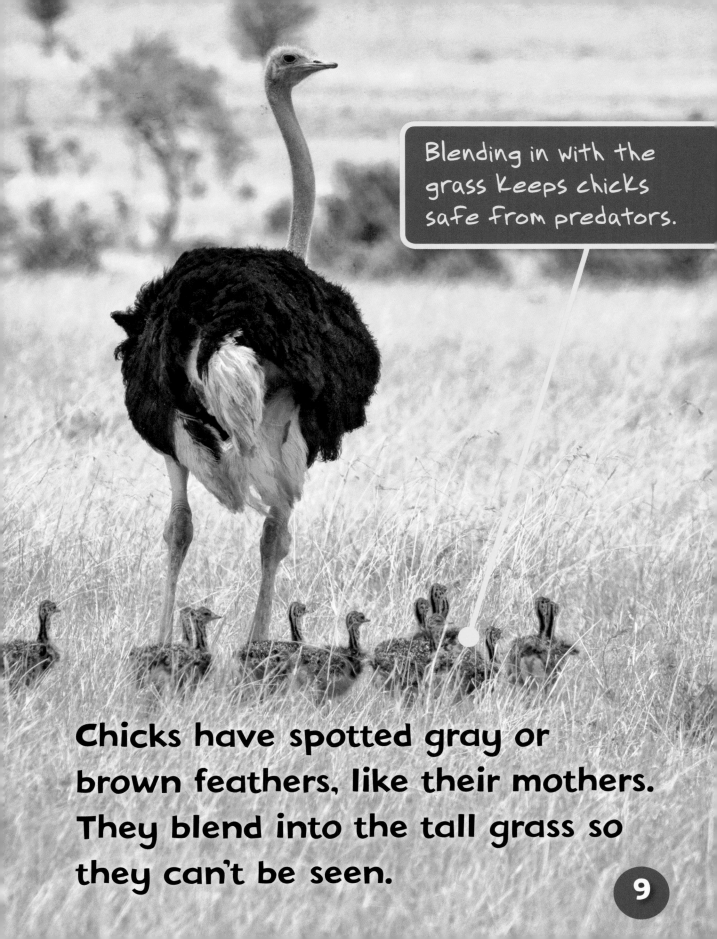

Blending in with the grass keeps chicks safe from predators.

Chicks have spotted gray or brown feathers, like their mothers. They blend into the tall grass so they can't be seen.

Growing and Changing

Chicks leave the pit a few days after they hatch. They stay with their parents and other adults in a herd.

Ostrich parents lead their chicks to the herd.

Six to ten adult ostriches
live together in a herd.

Fifteen to forty chicks
are part of the herd.

A baby ostrich grows 1 foot (30 cm) each month for the first few months. By six months old, a baby ostrich is almost as tall as its parents.

Ostrich chicks grow quickly in their first year.

Ostriches' feet help them run fast.

Ostriches are the only birds with two toes on each foot. Most birds have three or four toes. Ostriches' legs and feet are perfect for running. These big birds cannot fly.

Chicks run with the herd to strengthen their legs.

By one month old, chicks can run as fast as their parents.

Chicks begin running at a young age.

Ostriches can run up to **45** miles (78 kilometers) per hour. Ostriches' wings help them balance and change direction when running.

Ostriches are the world's fastest bird on land.

Chicks find shelter from the hot sun and rain under adults' wings.

Chicks cool off under their parents' wings.

Adults have *big, soft* feathers.

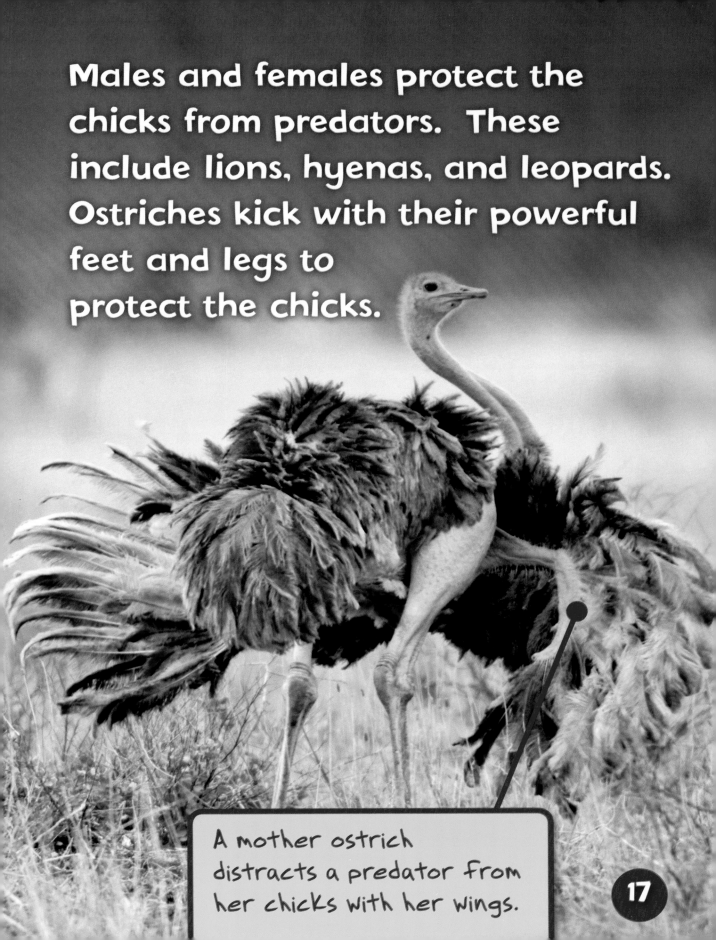

Males and females protect the chicks from predators. These include lions, hyenas, and leopards. Ostriches kick with their powerful feet and legs to protect the chicks.

A mother ostrich distracts a predator from her chicks with her wings.

Let's Eat!

Most chicks hatch in the rainy season when there are lots of plants and bugs to eat. A male from the herd protects them and teaches them how to eat.

A male watches for predators while the chicks look for food.

Ostriches are curious animals. Chicks will peck anything they see.

Ostriches search the grass and the bushes for food.

This ostrich munches on plants.

As they grow, chicks eat plants, roots, and seeds. They also eat insects, lizards, and other small creatures.

Ostriches gather in large groups at watering holes. They join other animals such as zebras and antelopes.

Many African animals gather at watering holes at once.

Ostriches have large eyes and long necks. If ostriches see a predator near a watering hole, they run.

Ostriches make a quick escape if they see a predator.

Ostriches also get water from the plants they eat. This helps them go for many days without drinking water.

Ostriches can reach leaves on tall bushes and trees.

Home in the Savanna

By one year old, ostriches weigh up to 350 pounds (150 kg). That is almost twice the weight of an average person.

Ostriches are big animals!

In about two to four years, ostriches will be ready to start their own families.

New ostrich families begin each rainy season.

Ostrich herds join together in flocks of fifty or more birds. They graze with other animals and take baths at watering holes.

A large group of ostriches gathers in a grassland.

An ostrich may live until it is forty or fifty years old. Chicks stay close to their parents. Then they grow up and the herd continues to grow.

Ostrich Life Cycle

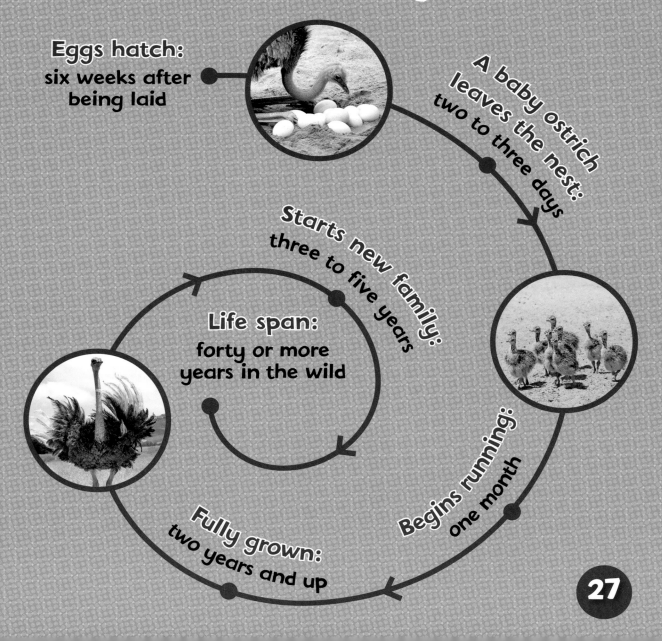

Eggs hatch:
six weeks after being laid

A baby ostrich leaves the nest:
two to three days

Starts new family:
three to five years

Life span:
forty or more years in the wild

Begins running:
one month

Fully grown:
two years and up

Habitat in Focus

- Ostriches live in savannas and some areas of the desert.

- The savanna has a rainy season, when it is hot and humid. It also has a long dry season.

- Savannas are also home to many plants, bugs, and lizards that make good food for ostriches.

- Grazing cattle and hunting have shrunk ostriches' habitats. Wild ostriches are found only in Africa.

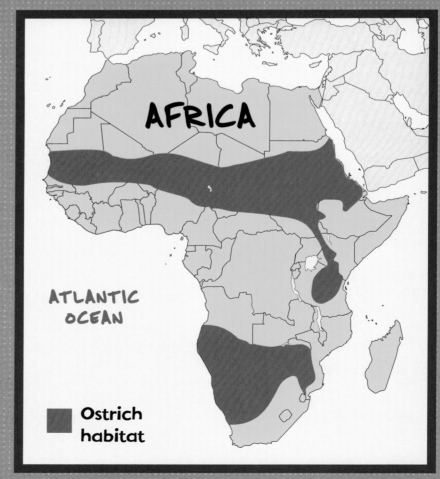

AFRICA

ATLANTIC OCEAN

Ostrich habitat

Fun Facts

- Ostriches have soft, fluffy feathers on their backs. They have short bristly feathers on their necks and heads. Their legs have no feathers.

- Ostrich eyes are almost 2 inches (5 cm) wide.

- Ostriches have long, thick eyelashes to protect their eyes from sand and wind.

Glossary

chick: the name for some baby birds

graze: to feed on grasses and plants

hatch: to break through the shell of an egg

hyena: a large animal of Africa that attacks and kills other animals

pit: the name for the hole or nest where ostriches lay their eggs

predator: an animal that hunts and kills other animals for food

Further Reading

Enchanted Learning: Ostrich
http://www.enchantedlearning.com
/subjects/birds/printouts/Ostrichcoloring.shtml

Kalman, Bobbie. *Baby Birds.* New York: Crabtree, Publishing Company, 2008.

Lunis, Natalie. *Ostrich: The World's Biggest Bird.* New York: Bearport Publishing, 2007.

Maynard, Thane. *Ostriches.* Chanhassen, MN: Child's World, 2007.

National Geographic: Ostrich
http://animals.nationalgeographic.com/animals /birds/ostrich

Silverman, Buffy. *Can You Tell an Ostrich from an Emu?* Minneapolis: Lerner Publications, 2012.

Index

chicks, 8, 9, 10, 11, 14, 16, 17, 18, 19, 20, 27

eggs, 4, 5, 6, 7, 27

feathers, 6, 9, 16
feet, 4, 13, 17
food, 18, 20

growth, 12, 20, 27

hatching, 4, 8, 10, 18, 27
herd, 10, 11, 14, 18, 26, 27

life cycle, 27
life span, 27

necks, 7, 22

predators, 17, 22

running, 13, 14, 15, 22, 27

size, 5, 8, 12, 24

water, 23
watering holes, 21, 22, 26
wings, 15, 16

Photo Acknowledgments

The images in this book are used with the permission of: © netsuthep/Shutterstock Images, pp. 2, 5; © fullempty/Shutterstock Images, pp. 4, 27 (top); © Elizabeth Hoffmann/iStock/Thinkstock, pp. 6, 24, 27 (bottom left), 31; © Stacey Ann Alberts/ Shutterstock Images, pp. 7, 27 (bottom right); © Sergei25/Shutterstock Images, pp. 8, 23; © moodboard/Thinkstock, p. 9; © Ann and Steve Toon/NHPA/Photoshot/Newscom, p. 10; © John Michael Evan Potter/Shutterstock Images, p. 11; © Cristian Zamfir/ Shutterstock Images, p. 12; © Dam Smith/Shutterstock Images, p. 13; © Photocreo Michal Bednarek/Shutterstock Images, p. 14; © John Carnemolla/iStock/Thinkstock, p. 15; © Jorens-Belde/Picture Alliance/Arco Images G/Newscom, p. 16; © Ariadne Van Zandbergen/Alamy, p. 17; © Simon G/Shutterstock Images, p. 18; © Lindsay Basson/ Shutterstock Images, p. 19; © Catfish Photography/Shutterstock Images, p. 20; © Hannes Thirion/iStock/Thinkstock, p. 21; © ilovezion/Shutterstock Images, p. 22; © Angelo Lano/iStock/Thinkstock, p. 25; © Andrea Willmore/iStock/Thinkstock, p. 26; Red Line Editorial, 28; © anankkml/iStock/Thinkstock, p. 30.

Front cover: © Mitsuaki Iwago/Minden Pictures/Getty Images

Main body text set in Johann Light 30/36.